EN DIVINA LUZ

THE PENITENTE MORADAS OF NEW MEXICO

PHOTOGRAPHS BY CRAIG VARJABEDIAN

ESSAY BY MICHAEL WALLIS

FOREWORD BY HERMANO FELIPE ORTEGA
AFTERWORD BY HERMANO CHARLES M. CARRILLO

University of New Mexico Press   Albuquerque

LIBRARY OF CONGRESS CATALOGING-IN-PUBLICATION DATA

EN DIVINA LUZ: THE PENITENTE MORADAS OF NEW MEXICO / PHOTOGRAPHS

BY CRAIG VARJABEDIAN; ESSAY BY MICHAEL WALLIS; FOREWORD BY FELIPE

ORTEGA; AFTERWORD BY CHARLES M. CARRILLO. — 1ST ED.

P.   CM.

INCLUDES BIBLIOGRAPHICAL REFERENCES.

ISBN 0-8263-1547-X

I. HERMANOS PENITENTES. 2. MORADAS—NEW MEXICO. 3. HISPANIC

AMERICAN CATHOLICS—NEW MEXICO—RELIGIOUS LIFE. 4. NEW MEXICO

—RELIGIOUS LIFE AND CUSTOMS.

I. VARJABEDIAN, CRAIG, 1957-   . II. WALLIS, MICHAEL, 1945-

BX810.H57D58   1994

267'.182789—DC20   94-20671

CIP

DESIGNED BY KRISTINA KACHELE

PRINTED BY LITHO SPECIALTIES, ST. PAUL, MINNESOTA

BOUND BY MIDWEST EDITIONS, MINNEAPOLIS, MINNESOTA

PHOTOGRAPH PAGE I: *Clouds, late afternoon thunderstorm near Carrizozo, 1986.*

PHOTOGRAPH PAGE III: *Rio Chama, early morning light, late autumn, 1985.*

PHOTOGRAPH PAGE V: *Tunyo: The Black Mesa, San Ildefonso Pueblo, late afternoon light, autumn, 1986.*

FRONTISPIECE: *Three crosses representing the good thief, Jesus Christ, and the bad thief, evening light, early autumn, 1993.*

This book is dedicated to
LOS HERMANOS DE
LA FRATERNIDAD PIADOSA DE
NUESTRO PADRE JESÚS NAZARENO
whose hands have shaped these moradas,
whose lives have filled them,
and whose spirit has kept the flame alive,

and to the memory of
DR. THOMAS R. LYONS
and to his surviving wife and partner
MARGIL LYONS
without whom this book and this journey
would not have been made.

Contents

Foreword

The memory of our Sisters and Brothers of La Cofradía de Nuestro Padre Jesús Nazareno* who have gone from this earthly morada to the heavenly one lives on every time the alabados are sung. In particular, I think of the alabado "*San Pedro me abra las Puertas, para entrar a su morada*—May St. Peter open unto me the gates so I may enter into His dwelling place." One Brother used to sing that alabado with great feeling, reverence, and understanding and to this day I can still hear him explaining the richness of this alabado and in particular the meaning of the word *morada.* Thus early on, my consciousness of being a Brother in this confraternity was molded by such songs and by the insights that words like *morada* conveyed.

The morada to me is not simply any dwelling place, it is my home. I live in Albuquerque most of the time, and in the past I have been as far away as the East Coast and the deep South. Yet every time I return to the village

---

* Some have said that the official title of our "Brotherhood" is La Fraternidad Piadosa de Nuestro Padre Jesús Nazareno. At our chapter house we have always used the word *Cofradía* (confraternity) instead of *Fraternidad* (fraternity) when we speak about our society. I believe it to be more correct because it acknowledges women as part of our organization. Thus we speak about ourselves as *Cofrados* and *Cofradas* (men and women who belong to a confraternity).

and to the chapter house, which we call la morada, I know I am home. I have come back to where my soul's roots were planted. Some years when I could not return for the Holy Season of Lent, I died a thousand deaths because I knew my Brothers and Sisters in my chapter house would be there praying for me and all the others who were absent. All the members of the chapter house, both men and women, are truly my brothers and sisters, and our Father is Jesus and our Mother is Mary. Men usually belong as regular members *(los regulares)* and sometimes both men and women belong to this confraternity as auxiliary members *(los y las auxiliares)*.

The Catholic religion teaches that Jesus Christ is Lord and Brother, but in our chapter houses Jesus is akin to the founding father of a Catholic religious order and thus He is given the title of Father. The long tradition in the Catholic Church that proclaims the Blessed Virgin Mary as both the Mother of the Church and consequently our Mother is kept alive within this confraternity. The morada symbolizes the unity that most Christians would like to feel in the larger churches of Christendom but seldom do.

Throughout all of New Mexico, and up into Colorado, in small Hispanic villages (with Moorish, Jewish, Spanish, Mexican, and Native American roots and now with other western European ancestors such as the French in northern New Mexico and the Irish in southern New Mexico), there stand sentinels of our ancient and living faith in the form of the dwelling places, the moradas, those buildings that resemble a simple home. Each one of them is the place where God has pitched his tent to dwell among us. For the faith of my people teaches us that the dwelling places that God has prepared for us in His Celestial Kingdom are mirrored in this earthly existence in these most sacred of structures. These are not the cathedrals of Europe, nor the massive Mexican temples of the ancient ones, just simple unadorned dwellings that reflect some of the Native American religious mentality which has created the Pueblo kivas. The moradas might seem unable to convey, in and of themselves, the magnificence of heaven. But when you are inside you can sense the joy and peace of heaven that surpass all earthly beauty. Mystically, the morada is transformed into the most beautiful of buildings on this earth, though no words will ever convey this.

This sense is also present in the traditional religious images of our ancestors, called bultos and retablos. To the Mexican and French clergy and in particular to the prelates who were sent to New Mexico, these holy images were unworthy of being used in Catholic worship. Therefore many images were destroyed and then others were sold away. But for those of us who can sense the mystical reality they portray, these images depict our brothers and sisters who have won the fight and are now in heaven. The Greek Orthodox Church calls these images icons, meaning "windows into Heaven." So too moradas are extraordinary windows through which we can see into heaven, and the reality they represent cannot be measured by human standards.

Rarely does one find someone from another culture or for that matter from another religion who fully understands the significance of these works of art, whether santos or moradas. Yet Craig Varjabedian has been sent to all of us who will enjoy this book as a prophetic messenger from the Great Mystery, so that our eyes can be opened to see through his camera's lens what his heart has sensed all along—that moradas are the earthly images of the heavenly mansion. As Craig experienced a morada bathed in light, translucent and transcendent, *En Divina Luz,* he has captured that mystery on film. His photographs could simply be another attempt to catalog our dwelling places as was attempted in the past, if his approach from the very beginning were not to convey to the whole world what he had felt in his heart and seen through his eyes. For Craig, being wonderfully artistic, has revealed in his photographs the feeling of otherworldliness and of heaven that our moradas evoke. He has captured it for us on film much as through their ancient art the santeros, by painting their holy images, were able to show us our ancestors in heaven.

After viewing some of Craig's early photographs, several of us brothers, for various reasons, encouraged him to make these pictures. We knew full well that his efforts would be invaluable to us Brothers of Our Father Jesus for preserving the memory of our earthly and heavenly dwellings. Craig decided that these pictures should be shared with all and a book was to be part of the outcome of his years of making photographs.

Craig enlisted the help of author Michael Wallis to complete the book with printed text. Michael's written word interprets the alabados sung and the liturgies prayed inside the moradas and makes them resound in our hearts like a heavenly music we hear within. His words embody the feelings that are evoked inside the chapter house, in particular inside the oratorio or chapel where we gather for prayer. Since Craig photographed none of the interiors of the moradas, we invite you to enter into our dwelling places through Michael's words and poetry and to live and pray there with us. Michael has not written about the private rituals of the regulares, since they are open only to the initiated. Yet with reverence for those private rituals, he has explained to the best of his ability that these rituals are not to be seen as horrendous torture (which they are not) but instead, acts of love for a Divine Spouse. It is our hope that Michael's words will combine with Craig's photographs in this book to bring about a reverence and respect for these seemingly lowly buildings our ancestors left as reminders of the greater realities within each one of us and far beyond this world.

A final word: our moradas are physically divided into two main sections, the first being the oratorio and the second the living quarters where we eat, sleep, pray, listen to exhortations, discuss, and study both our tradition and Catholic theology. When you are invited to partake of the simple, heart-touching rituals of this Cofradía, you will probably share this experience in an oratorio. But ultimately the two sections are one, and you will find that you too have entered the heavenly dwelling place where Jesus Christ is our Father and Lord and the Blessed Virgin Mary is our Mother and Lady.

Some of my Brothers and Sisters, and perhaps even others, might take offense at this book, but it was never my nor the photographer's nor author's intention to create disharmony. My prayer is that through this book we Sisters and Brothers in this confraternity and all who partake of this book might see the moradas as a treasure left to all men and women.

La Paz de Nuestro Señor Jesucristo sea siempre entre todos nosotros—May the Peace of Our Lord Jesus Christ be among us always.

HERMANO FELIPE ORTEGA
Hermano de la Morada de
Nuestra Señora de Guadalupe
January 1994

Then God said, "Let there be light,"
and there was light.
GENESIS 1:3 (NAB)

Upon the Threshold of the Sacred

I

Everlasting sunlight, pure as angel's breath, spills from the heavens, melting over the New Mexican landscape and the plastered adobe walls of the morada. Stalks of light, the first element of creation, sent from the fiery yellow-white star, seep through halos of clouds shrouding mountain peaks where winds are born and rainbows hide. Some clouds break away. Like mounds of singed meringue, they become the shadow of God. The clouds drift close to the earth as though to have a better look at the Chama River Valley village below before dancing over the surrounding canyons and hills studded with piñon, cholla, and chamiso.

It is April, the fourth month of the Christian year. Its name is from the Latin verb meaning "to open," as the buds are beginning to do in the fields, gardens, and orchards. Still early in spring—the season of birth and renewal that bridges the March equinox and the June solstice—winter's grip lingers throughout northern New Mexico. Yet the fragrance of the awakening earth is powerful.

Just outside the morada, a procession of men, women, and children from the village treads across the wild grasses. Clumps of alfalfa, its tender shoots pushing from the frosty ground toward the sun, are crushed under-foot, releasing a potent aroma. Believed to have been used as forage longer than any other plant, alfalfa was cultivated by ancient Persians and Greeks. Spanish explorers and settlers carried alfalfa to South America and Mexico. Eventually it found its way to this land to thrive, both wild and cultivated, as a feed crop and as a renewer of the soil. Spawned by seed that may have arrived windblown or clinging to a muddy shoe, the slender alfalfa stems outside the morada will survive to produce purple blossoms loaded with nectar for the bees. Deep taproots take in water and nutrients. Much like the Hispano people who inhabit this land, the clusters of alfalfa are an-chored firmly in the earth.

The villagers have already fallen in love with the new season. Soft wind caresses them as they proceed one by one through the open weather-stained door and enter the morada. These are people of strong faith who live in communion with the earth and the light. They understand the lan-guage of the clouds, and they absolutely trust what they find in nature.

One man pauses before entering the morada. He turns his face toward the sunlight, and the whisper of a smile appears on his lips. *"Créanse del aire,"* says the man to no one in particular. *"Créanse del aire."*

It is a *dicho,* or proverb, that affirms instant belief without thinking. Just as he disappears inside, he says it once again: *"Créanse del aire."*

Believe in the wind.

II

Moradas are sculpted from the soil. Like so much of the architecture that makes up the Native American pueblos and the necklace of Hispano ham-lets scattered across northern New Mexico, many moradas are built of adobe.

Adobe is a Spanish word of Arabic origin given to the plastered bricks fashioned from handfuls of La Santa Madre Tierra, "the Holy Mother Earth." This building material dates back thousands of years to early Egypt and Babylonia.

Builders dig their fingers into the loose mantle of mineral and matter and feel the energy of the earth. They mix sandy clay with water and some straw to hold the mud together. They can tell by the feel of the loose batter when it is ready to be placed into wooden forms to shape adobes that will be dried in the sun.

The bricks serve as a form of memory. They furnish evidence of the past. When the plaster falls off old buildings, the exposed adobes may reveal traces of deer which had come in late spring to nibble the straw in the newly made bricks, leaving hoofprints frozen in time. The etched palms of generations long gone and bits of animal bone and rock give texture to the thick walls.

FIGURE 1. *Corner of abandoned morada and edge of storm clouds, late afternoon, summer, 1993.*

On this April afternoon, the procession of villagers has entered a morada built in about 1900 on a foundation of native stone. The morada is situated at the end of a terraced field where many of the genízaros settled in the middle of the eighteenth century. The converted descendants of Native American captives ransomed from nomadic tribes by Spanish authorities, these settlers built their village over the site of a long-deserted Tewa pueblo ruin. Although not built by Native Americans, this morada was historically called La Morada del Moqui, "the morada of the Hopi," by the people of the village. Through the years the older version of that changed to Moque,

3 ✠

the name most people now use. Besides lore of the genízaros, stories about youngsters who were taken by los Indios are still passed down from generation to generation like sacred family heirlooms.

✛ ✛ ✛

Tío Ben was ninety-six years old when he died. He used to tell us stories about his grandfather who was just a boy of about ten years of age when some Navajos came and took him. He was with another boy from the village and they went to get some burros from near the creek, not far from where the morada called El Moque was built many years later. The other boy was able to escape, but they grabbed Tío Ben's grandfather and they rode far away.

He was raised to be an Indian, but eventually he came back. Some soldiers traded with the Indians, and they saw the Spanish boy and asked him where he was from and if he wanted to go home, and he said he did. So they brought him back here to the village. He was sixteen years old when he returned.

WIFE OF AN HERMANO

✛ ✛ ✛

Like the many moradas that remain in northern New Mexico and southern Colorado, El Moque has its own particular character. In scale and design the elongated boxlike adobe resembles a village house, especially the older Hispano homes built on the frontier. Their windowless facades and unbroken walls offered the genízaro settlers sanctuary from Ute, Navajo, or Apache warriors who roamed this land before the arrival of the Spaniards.

The earthen structure's appearance is fitting because most Hispanic scholars believe the word *morada* was adapted from the Spanish noun for dwelling, or from the verb *morar,* "to live or dwell." Still, despite its domestic facade, the morada is purely ecclesiastical in origin and religious in purpose.

Moradas are inspired edifices. They are holy places.

Moradas serve as chapter houses for a lay religious brotherhood found exclusively in this region that is formally known as La Fraternidad Piadosa de Nuestro Padre Jesús Nazareno, or the Pious Fraternity of Our Father Jesus the Nazarene. Members of this Hermandad (Brotherhood) or Cofradía (Confraternity) are commonly called Los Hermanos Penitentes, the Penitent Brothers, or simply Los Hermanos.

The history of this lay Catholic organization is deeply rooted in colonial New Mexico. Some writers have attempted to link Los Hermanos Penitentes with the Third Order of Saint Francis—the Brothers and Sisters of Penance—established by Saint Francis of Assisi in 1221. Others claim that the Brotherhood is connected to the Holy Week penance carried out in this region in 1598 by the Spanish colonizer Don Juan de Oñate and the Franciscans who followed him. But most scholars now agree that the Hermandad in New Mexico did not formally organize until sometime between 1776 and 1833. This was the period when the Catholic church in the area was in shambles and, relative to the region's growing Hispanic population, only a few priests could be found to provide for the people's spiritual needs. The lay brotherhood filled this ecclesiastical void.

The Brotherhood's origins may always remain shrouded in mystery and their ceremonies may frequently be misconstrued, but their importance to the continuation of the cultural heritage of New Mexico and the Catholic Church can never be denied. A critical ingredient in the preservation of the Brotherhood's social and religious beliefs is their moradas.

The faith and devotion of the Hermanos are quietly revealed in their moradas. Joined as one in their chapels, the Brothers relish the flavor of life as they pray and sing and speak to saints and angels and dead ancestors.

✠   ✠   ✠

I have much feeling for my Brothers. We are all pieces of one another. We are like the adobes that make our moradas. An adobe brick by itself is not much good, but when it joins with others it has purpose.

AN HERMANO

III

On this Wednesday afternoon of Holy Week, Semana Santa, the climax of the Lenten season is drawing near. Almost two dozen people have taken their places inside the "chapel room," or *oratorio,* of the morada called El Moque. Some of the older ones shuffle to benches along the smooth walls, while most of the villagers stand with hands folded, heads bowed. At the front of the room, near the altar where saints reside, are several of the Hermanos, erect as soldiers as they chant timeless hymns known as alabados.

The flames of the morada candles seem to sing along with the Brothers. God dwells in the glow of the candlelight.

✠   ✠   ✠

All that came to be had life in him and that life was the light of men, a light that shines in the dark, a light that darkness could not overpower.

JOHN 1:4-5 (JB)

✠   ✠   ✠

Outside, the wind grows so strong that it sounds as though it might become visible. The wind has a life all its own. It is the spring wind that carves snow and sand, the wind that scatters seeds, the wind that clears the skies of poisons. It is the wind that flushes out the last of winter. It is the wind of hope and revival.

The wind rubs against the adobe walls as even more clouds rush overhead. Unlike the constant mountains huddled in the distance, the clouds are nameless monuments, always changing in form and color. These are not the massive Old Testament clouds that congregate on summer days and hover high above the plains. These are the clouds of April, young clouds that will wash the mountains, fill the rivers, and allow the grass, flowers, and crops to arise from the earth. The clouds roll by, and the shadows shift inside the morada. Soon the shadows fade, and then they vanish.

Sunlight oozing through the windows blends with the radiance of the candles. The chapel is flooded with light. The light is a harbinger of the spring, of the genesis of weather. All eyes can see that the light is celestial. It has become divine light—*divina luz.*

☩   ☩   ☩

Hoy aclaman los cofrados,
aclaman aquí esta luz,
para llevar en el pecho
a Nuestro Padre Jesús

Today the brothers call upon,
call upon this light
so as to carry in the heart
Our Father Jesus.

FROM AN ALABADO
Por Ser Mi Divina Luz

After more than an hour of kneeling and standing, reciting the rosary, and praying the stations of the cross, the Lenten pilgrims adjourn. Guests are invited to share coffee and sugar cookies, bizcochitos. During the service, it became warm inside the morada, so most people take their leave. The cool air is refreshing. Those who have not given up tobacco for Lent light up cigarettes.

Many of the Brothers have come from far away, some from as far as Colorado and Utah. Several of them live in Albuquerque or Santa Fe. They shake hands and embrace relatives and old friends they have not seen for a long time. It is an annual homecoming.

The afternoon air is soothing, and the fragrance of the crushed alfalfa still hangs in the wind. White-faced cows, attracted by the smell, have come to eat their share. Some Brothers chase the cows away. Villagers and guests head for cars or pickup trucks parked nearby. A few walk down the road to their homes.

The apricot trees have just blossomed. The irrigation ditch, or acequia, has been cleaned out. Soon, water will be flowing to the fields. Cycles of life will continue in the path of divine light.

IV

"I am the light of the world. No follower of mine shall ever walk in the darkness; no, he shall possess the light of life."

JOHN 8:12 (NAB)

The Brothers leave El Moque and go to the other side of the Chama River Valley village to a much older morada named Morada del Alto, or "morada on the hill." Built between 1820 and 1850, it is one of the oldest surviving moradas in New Mexico.

Several of the Hermanos believe their village has two moradas because the membership of their first morada grew too large for the building. Still others suggest that the newer morada was the result of a long-forgotten squabble that could not be reconciled. They say that around the turn of this century, dissident members of the Brotherhood who became embroiled in the dispute left the morada "on the hill" and ultimately built El Moque as their new communal meetinghouse. Hardly anyone from the village accepts the explanation that the split came about because of political differences among the Brothers, resulting in one morada for Democrats and the other for Republicans, as some scholars have theorized.

Despite periods of inactivity when the Brotherhood's membership has been sparse, both the moradas have remained special to the local people. Both the moradas are loved. But to the Brothers of the village, the morada "on the hill" is an extra special place. Like the Brothers themselves, this morada has endured despite many trials and travails. Not everyone respects the cultural and spiritual importance of the Hermanos and their moradas. Thieves and vandals have taken a toll on moradas throughout northern New Mexico and southern Colorado.

In 1972, during a time when more than two dozen moradas were violated, looters made off with scores of religious sculptures at El Moque. Through the years, sacred objects also were taken from Morada del Alto. In 1980, an accidental fire broke out in that morada, destroying some of the

FIGURE 2. *Morada with three crosses after the fire (taken the day after), afternoon, autumn, 1992.*

artifacts and a large section of the roof. The Brothers did not give up. They raised money and rebuilt.

On a bright July Sabbath just three years after the flames were extinguished, the Brothers rededicated their restored morada. Nearly two thousand people turned out for the observance, including the Archbishop of Santa Fe and local dancers who symbolized the village's genízaro heritage. Almost one hundred Hermanos, representing several moradas, also came to the village to mark the occasion.

Sadly, the faith and endurance of the Brothers were tested yet again. A new outrage, the most difficult of all to bear, tried the mettle of even the most stalwart Hermanos.

In the early hours of September 17, 1992, the Morada del Alto was desecrated by a person or persons unknown. So vicious were the cruel acts against the chapel that many villagers and Brothers believed it was carried out by an evil force that came directly from hell.

As the villagers slept, the unknown force first vandalized and then set the historic morada ablaze. The inferno collapsed ceilings and walls and destroyed historic pieces of furniture, rugs, and irreplaceable works of religious art. Satanic images—a trio of sixes and a devil's pentagram—had been sprayed in red paint on the scorched walls that survived.

Not satisfied with desecrating the morada, the transgressors also mangled several of the Brothers' revered santos. Others were stolen. Some of them were later found—broken and burned—in an arroyo. State police investigators recovered more of the santos from beneath a bridge.

⊹ ⊹ ⊹

Our santos are not just beautiful wooden figures. Nor are they simply works of art. To us, they are like our family. We have respect for them. We grew up with these saints. They protect us and help us and listen to our prayers. The older santos were carved by our ancestors, and the newer ones were created by our fellow Hermanos. They are made from the wood that grows on this land. They are painted with the natural pigments that come from the Mother Earth we love.

AN HERMANO

⊹ ⊹ ⊹

The day after the holocaust, the Brothers of the village climbed the gentle hill and went to the ruins of their morada. Together, they knelt in the warm ashes and prayed. With tears streaming down their faces, they pledged to rebuild the adobe walls and to fix the battered and scarred saints. Then they rolled up their sleeves and went to work.

Endless wheelbarrows of debris were removed. Tons of ashes and rubble were carted away. Trucks carried hundreds of thirty-pound adobes to the hill, along with fresh vigas, peeled ponderosa pine and spruce logs each as big around as a man, for the ceiling beams. New wooden canales—water spouts—were made for the roof. Santeros, the makers of wooden saints, worked at a feverish pace to mend the scorched figures or to create new ones to take their place.

The Brothers' goal was to resurrect their chapel in time for Lenten services in the spring. They were successful. Their prayers were answered.

✝   ✝   ✝

Our morada was rebuilt in only a few months because we went there and prayed and made our promises, but also because we forgave those who brought that destruction. In our hearts, we had to forgive: otherwise, every single brick we laid would have been a negative brick, every handful of plaster would have been bitter.

We saw that our morada returned to Mother Earth and became the fertilizer for our growth. A new morada came from those ashes. The foundation was left, and that was good. If you have a foundation, then you can build from there. The same is true with our culture. As long as we keep our foundation, then we will survive.

AN HERMANO

Sometimes we are given a cross to bear, and this was ours. The evil that was perpetrated here did not defeat us.

AN HERMANO

VI

Inside the Morada del Alto, the chapel that rose like a phoenix from its own ashes, the Brothers rest and prepare for the evening rosary service and the rest of the activities of Holy Week.

After six months of hard work through a harsh mountain winter, they are pleased that their morada has been restored. They recall the recent words of an old Spanish proverb repeated by a Catholic priest who came to give his blessing. "*No hay mal que por bien no venga. There is no evil from which good cannot come,*" the priest told the Brothers. "This evil is going to yield a harvest of good." They know he is correct.

One Hermano fills an enameled kettle with water and brews a pot of *chamiso hediondo* tea over the stack of wood burning in the fogón, a small corner fireplace. This Brother resides in Santa Fe with his wife and children. He is studying for a doctorate in anthropology. He also is an accomplished and acclaimed *santero,* as are several of the other Hermanos who belong to this morada chapter.

✠ ✠ ✠

My family is of genízaro lineage and first settled in northern New Mexico during the mid-1700s. My wife's family was among the original settlers of the village with two moradas located in the Chama River valley. I am a member in good standing in the Brotherhood, as were my forefathers, yet as is true of many Brothers of my generation, I no longer live in the village of my ancestors.

Still, I always return to the morada. The morada is a symbol of continuity, a reminder that those who went before us made many sacrifices to maintain something for succeeding generations.

AN HERMANO

FIGURE 3. *Patterns of the Brotherhood. Traditional New Mexico retablo. Clockwise from upper left: Santa Librada, El Espírítu Santo, San Acacio, Arma Christi, San Ignacio de Loyola, San Francisco de Asís, San Juan Nepomuceno, El Sagrador Corazón y las Cinco Llagas, (center) Nuestro Señor de Esquípulas.*

✠ ✠ ✠

Steaming cups of the pungent tea are passed around, and another Brother enters the morada. Born in this New Mexican village, as were his ancestors

FIGURE 4. *Rosary, matraca, cross of wood, and straw appliqué.*

for more than two centuries, the man, in his mid-forties, lives with his family in Albuquerque. He works for the state highway department, attends Sunday Mass at a large church, and coaches Little League baseball. Like so many of the Hermanos, he has also been blessed with talent as a skilled artisan. His exquisite straw and cornhusk inlay crosses grace homes and museums throughout the world.

He squats near the fireplace. In the glow of the flames, he takes up his few tools and without a word, he begins to create. Instead of a delicate straw crucifix, the Brother is preparing to make a *matraca,* a wooden clacker or cog rattle used by the Brothers in place of bells during their religious services, especially the Good Friday ceremonies.

The Brother will transform an old fruit crate into a *matraca* that will be used for many years to come. He measures the panels, marking the dimensions with a stub of pencil. A pocketknife and coping saw slice the wood into proportions that the Brother will fit together with a notched cylinder on the handle.

As he works, the other Brothers talk among themselves.

One of the Brothers stands smiling at the rest of them. He is in his early sixties and is the older brother of the man making the *matraca.* He holds a *cuaderno,* a small book filled with alabados, prayers, and the Brotherhood's rules. It is very old. The marks from the hands that held this book many years before stain its worn cover. He handles the book very carefully, as if it were a living thing.

☩   ☩   ☩

Every year when we get together for Holy Week and other times, I realize that we have lost the memory of many of the things that took place during the time of our grandfathers.

I am very involved in teaching other Brothers the traditions of the past. I want them to understand that we have a rich history which needs to be recorded. Part of that history is the history of our buildings—the moradas of our villages.

AN HERMANO

FIGURE 5. *Pito, cuaderno, divisa (badge).*

☩   ☩   ☩

Around this Brother's neck is a black cotton bandanna rolled into a tight loop. It is drawn together with a slide the man carved from bone on which he depicted Our Lady of Guadalupe.

From one of the oldest families in the region, the Brother enjoys the traditional Spanish art of bone carving. He makes turtles, owls, and religious figures. Mostly, he carves eagles—eagles that look very much like rising phoenix birds. Pieces of nails and bits of turquoise are used for the eyes. He

FIGURE 6. *Shepherd's ivory*

carves the leg bones of sheep, elk, or deer, working only with files and a razor-sharp knife. The neckerchief slides, tool handles, and other carvings he makes are called "shepherd's ivory."

The Brother explains that most shepherds still wear carved bones with their neckerchiefs. His father herded sheep and used to do such carving. Once his father made a whistle from a bear's tooth. The Brother has another bone carving that his late father made, and he uses some of the tools his father gave to him.

The man does not want to use any sort of modern tools. He wants to know the same feeling of working with the blades and the bones that his father and the others before him had when they carved. He does not care how long the carving takes. This is a man who does not wish to be in a hurry. He is interested in doing everything well, even if it takes longer. Like so many of his Brothers, he also is a man who values his past as he makes the most of the present.

✛   ✛   ✛

Some change is healthy, but sometimes change can be ruinous. We have to celebrate our history and embrace our traditions, but we must also continue to live in the here and now. There needs to be balance.

AN HERMANO

VII

According to the calendar, the season is supposed to be spring, but the weather remains unpredictable in northern New Mexico. Snow showers are known to occur even in late May.

Outside the rejuvenated Morada del Alto on this Holy Wednesday, Miércoles Santo, the bruised sky yields a scattering of enormous snow-flakes. Not the result of a full-blown storm, they are merely relics of the languishing winter. Slowly drifting toward earth through the slanted rays of the retreating sun, the swollen flakes come to rest in the hair and beards of the Brothers.

As the men make their way to supper at the home of the Hermano who carves shepherd's ivory, their moist dark eyes reflect the first silent stars of the evening—drops of divine light. In the heavens above New Mexico and the valley of the Río Chama, the Big Dipper wheels high in the north. Sirius—the Dog Star and brightest in the night sky—flashes and twinkles. Later, the constellation called Orion is due to make an appearance, low in the west below the flow of the Milky Way.

The Brother's home where the members of the morada gather for food and fellowship is only a few miles west of the village. It is among the houses, barns, and sheds making up Barranco, meaning "the ravine," as the locals in this part of Río Arriba County know the small farming community.

Several of the morada's officers, elected from among the initiated members in good standing, Los Regulares, pull up chairs around the dining-room table. One of them happens to be the Hermano Mayor, or Elder Brother, who serves as the leader and servant of the morada.

A group of the general membership including a few young men who have just joined the Brotherhood, called Los Novicios, the novices, stand around the table sharing *cuadernos* and raising their voices in song. They will sing alabados while the first group eats. When they are finished, the Brothers will exchange places. At no time will the house be empty of song.

When the members of one group complete the meal, they pray and then stand as one. They bow from the waist to softly kiss the tabletop. Except for some anxious novices who have to be corrected gently by the Maestro (Teacher) de Novicios when they fumble with the old Spanish lyrics, the Brothers sit as serene as priests.

Their wives and daughters have laid out a fine dinner. There are plenty of enchiladas and stacks of freshly made flour tortillas. The women scurry about, bringing out more bowls of food and dishes of a special sprouted-wheat dessert, panocha, and a bread pudding known as *sopa.* Coffee cups do not remain empty for long.

This Lenten meal has been prepared especially for the Brothers, but it is clear that these women are not subjugated to stereotypical roles. They are women of the here and now. They also have a place in the life and the conduct of the morada. Although full membership traditionally is open only to males, females act as *auxiliadoras,* or auxiliaries, sometimes called *ayudantes,* or helpers. They prepare meals, help to clean and care for the morada and the santos, and tend to the sick. Often these women also assist at velorios—wakes or vigils—and with the various public processions and rituals. In some instances, morada chapters have been known to include women who use the name *Hermana,* or Sister, sometimes called *Mana,* used as a name of affection.

✠   ✠   ✠

Our Brotherhood is not just for men. It is for women and children too. Families have always been involved.

WIFE OF AN HERMANO

The Hermandad is much more inclusive than it is exclusive. I suspect that if somehow we could find records from here in New Mexico in the 1790s, we would discover that women were once equal participants in the moradas. There may have been a sexual division as far as labor and authority—that is a consequence of our history and how the world used to operate. But I still believe women had as much to say as men.

AN HERMANO

Many people do not realize that there were females in the Hermandad, but there definitely were. They were not just auxiliary members, but they were bona fide Penitentas. In one village, they even had their own morada and they carried out the same practices as the Hermanos. There were many Penitentas, and perhaps someday there will be again.

AN HERMANO

The carver of shepherd's ivory and his younger brother—the man who makes inlaid straw crosses and *matracas*—know all about Penitentas. Their mother was one.

When she was a young woman, no one dared deny that she was the best horseback rider in all of the village. It was said that she could ride like the wind. Her children remember her as a woman who could do everything a man could do, only she could do it much better. Married to a sheepherder who was gone much of the time tending his flocks, she raised two sons, five daughters, and three grandchildren and served her morada.

Our mother could sing us verses about the morada in a very profound way. She knew so much about the morada. She was filled with wisdom.

Since she was one of the Penitentas, I went to her when I was starting to think about joining the Hermandad. I wasn't quite ready, and she knew it in an instant.

I recall exactly what she told me. She said, "Mi hijo, espérate. Es un camino muy duro." (Wait, my son. It is a very difficult journey). I listened to her. She was my spiritual guide. She was the person who had taught me how to pray.

Finally, when I felt I was ready to join, I discussed it with my wife, and I went back to my mother. She said, "Mi hijo, es un camino muy duro pero si este es lo que quieres, estás listo." (My son, it is a difficult journey, but if this is what you really want, you are ready). And so I was. I, too, became part of the morada.

AN HERMANO

⊹   ⊹   ⊹

The two brothers' elderly mother died less than three weeks after the Morada del Alto was desecrated and burned. She did not live to see its restoration, but she died knowing that her morada would be brought back to life.

The woman's remains were reduced to ashes, just like her beloved morada. Now that the walls of the chapter house are fixed and the santos have returned, her sons and daughters know that the time has arrived to lay the woman to rest.

Later in April, after the Lenten observances, her family and the Brothers will go to the morada "on the hill." There they will honor their Hermana. They will bury a pine box containing her ashes beneath the floor of the altar. Crafted by her younger son and dovetailed without using a single nail or tack, the box will be plain but exquisite. Her name and the dates of her birth and death will be carved into a simple sandstone slab and laid at floor level over the grave.

Prayers will be offered and answered. Sweet tears will fall. Symmetry will have been recovered at the morada. Balance will have been achieved. The old Penitenta will be at peace in the adobe earth.

☩　☩　☩

De la tierra fui formado,
La tierra me ha de comer,
La tierra me ha sustentado,
Y al fin yo tierra ha de ser.

From the earth I was made,
And the earth shall eat me,
The earth has sustained me,
And at last earth I shall be also.

FROM AN ALABADO
Adios, Acompañamiento

VIII

Be on guard against performing religious acts for people to see. Otherwise expect no recompense from your heavenly Father.

Whenever you pray, go to your room, close your door, and pray to your Father in private. Then your Father, who sees what no man sees, will repay you.

MATTHEW 6:1, 6 (NAB)

IX

It is Holy Thursday, Jueves Santo. In scattered parts of southern Colorado and all across the northern New Mexican countryside, hundreds of the Hermanos are drawn to their moradas.

Throughout the Mora Valley, along the Río Chama and Río Grande, at the ancient villages dotting the High Road to Taos, in remote canyons and on peaceful hilltops, the Brothers are joined by their families and friends as they make their way to their cherished moradas. The Brothers come from every walk of life. Many toil in the land of their ancestors. Some live and work in large cities and towns.

They seek the company of other men and become Hermanos for a variety of reasons. Some join the Brotherhood because their fathers or grandfathers belonged to the morada. Perhaps an uncle—their favorite tío—might have been been a Brother. Or they decide to become involved because their mothers were Hermanas. Others become Brothers as an act of atonement or after they have vowed that if loved ones are spared from illness, they will pledge themselves to the service of the Hermandad. Regardless of background, occupation, or motives for joining, the Brothers' lives in the morada are founded on strong spiritual beliefs.

✠   ✠   ✠

We are all normal, everyday people. We are ranchers, we are farmers, we are physicians, we are students, we are everyone.

We get together to pray. We find that praying can be a form of penance.

And we go to our morada to be reminded of the life of Christ. We go not to be reminded necessarily of all the suffering, but of all the good that Christ did. We attempt to emulate the life of Christ, not just by word but through our actions. Not just during Lent, but every day of our lives. Not just with our Brothers, but with every other person we meet along the way.

AN HERMANO

✠   ✠   ✠

There are no age restrictions governing membership in the Brotherhood, although most moradas prefer their novices to be at least fourteen years old. Those seeking admission should be members in good standing of the Holy Mother Catholic Church and must have received the consent of their mothers or, if they are married, their spouses so as not to create conflict in the family.

A strict rite of passage is part of the experience for the uninitiated. There are rituals, instructions, and examinations to endure. Joining the Hermandad is not a matter to be taken lightly. Vows pledging privacy and loyalty to the morada are made for life. Every Brother retains intimate memories of how and when he became a part of his morada.

✠   ✠   ✠

I joined the Brotherhood in 1969. I was seventeen when I joined. I had seen many of my relatives become part of the Hermandad. I knew that it was part of the community and our identity as people of northern New Mexico.

I had wanted to become an Hermano since I was about ten or eleven, but my mother wouldn't let me join because it was a lifelong commitment.

She didn't think I was prepared, even though an uncle in our family was given to the morada when he was three years old and another boy was brought to the morada as an offering when he was five.

AN HERMANO

My grandmother was the last of the female Penitentas in our village. When my grandmother died, they gave her an entire Penitente funeral with everything that is done for an Hermano.

My earliest memory is of my grandmother carrying me in her arms on a wooden plank over an arroyo. She didn't trust me crossing that arroyo on my own. Every Holy Week, she'd hold me in her arms and we'd cross that arroyo to go pray the Stations of the Cross. Later, I realized the symbolism of our crossing that water. She physically and spiritually carried me across the perils so I could attend those holy services.

AN HERMANO

After I joined the Brotherhood, I found our rich heritage. When you're on the outside, you don't see the rich heritage. You only see it when you're completely inside the walls of the morada. That is when you begin to see many things in a different light.

AN HERMANO

I joined when I was a grandfather, but actually in my heart I had joined the Brothers long, long before that.

I first started following the Hermandad when I was ten years old. I would hear my uncles and others singing the alabados, and I thought those words were so very beautiful. My grandmother taught me what those words meant. I have never forgotten them.

AN HERMANO

X

To be a Penitente
is to be in love.

A WRITER

XI

Perched above the village, the Morada del Alto—the exalted adobe vessel that remains forever landlocked—is filled with Hermanos at prayer. Thin trails of piñon, juniper, and cottonwood smoke rise from the chimney into the brilliant blue sky. Villagers, friends, and family members gather outside the morada door, waiting for the Brothers to emerge. The flaming sun of Moses and the prophets, the same sun that was darkened by the death of Christ, faithfully climbs the heavens. At last Holy Friday—Viernes Santo—has arrived once again.

The vigils, processions, and dramatizations of Holy Thursday, all of the observances and prayers of the past forty days of Lent—La Cuaresma—that started with Ash Wednesday, Miércoles de Ceniza, leading up to Easter Sunday, Pascua Florida, will culminate this day, on this Good Friday.

At midmorning, Los Hermanos come forth from their morada. They are joined in procession by those outside, whose faces are as familiar to the Brothers as the hollyhocks that will bloom by their homes in the summer.

The time has come for one of the most moving rituals of La Semana Santa. It is El Encuentro, commemorating the meeting between Christ and the Blessed Virgin Mary on the path to Calvary. It is the Fourth Station of La Vía Crucis, the Way of the Cross.

In the lead are the Brothers and three young women, dressed all in black, with their heads shrouded. They slowly walk, bearing a bulto, a carved image, of the Holy Mother. As the somber procession makes three complete circles around the morada, the public guests fall in line. Each time the Brothers pass the three large crosses impaled in the earth at the far end of their morada, they reach out and gently touch the weathered wood and make the sign of the cross.

They make their way down the hill toward the center of the village. People come out of their houses to watch. The procession passes a long adobe wall. Behind it sits the empty home of a woman, now dead, who used to paint portraits of the surrounding landscape. In the garden, the descendants of flowers that the artist loved to paint are coming back to life. Soon, songbirds will nest in the tall cottonwoods.

The Good Friday pilgrims make footprints on the dirt road. Their hymns never cease. Men fire antique flintlock guns in the morning air as part of an ancient ritual to drive away any evil that might be lingering. The people are quiet when they halt at several intervals to kneel and recite the Stations of the Cross.

At the same time, another procession of Hermanos and villagers has left the morada called El Moque. They carry the carved image of Christ, swathed in purple cloth, hands bound.

The two groups advance toward each other in front of the village church. Hymns of the Passion are sung as the dressed images of Christ and the Blessed Virgin converge.

The sculpted figures are tipped forward, close together, symbolizing the final embrace between Christ and the Blessed Virgin Mary. A Mother bids farewell to her condemned Son.

It is a powerful scene, a moment that evokes great tenderness. Tears stream down the cheeks of almost every person there.

High above the village, a jet airplane's contrails stain the sky. The streaks of condensed water vapor and the plane hurtling through time and space contrast sharply with the scene below and the other places throughout this land where Brothers congregate. This land with an old soul.

☩   ☩   ☩

Adiós Hijo mío,
Adiós mi Señor,
Adiós de los cielos,
Adiós, Salvador.

Goodbye my Son,
Goodbye my Lord,
Goodbye from heaven,
Goodbye, Savior.

FROM AN ALABADO
Lloren Pecadores

XII

The focus of the Hermandad always has been and always will be the Passion and death of Jesus Christ.

Because of this, the Brothers are still greatly misunderstood and misrepresented. Their intimate acts of penance and devotion, carried out in private behind their morada walls, have been sensationalized by inflammatory reports from numerous authors, journalists, and historians. Many of the

accounts of the Brotherhood, especially those dealing with Lenten observances, paint grisly portraits of fanatical Hermanos engaged in masochistic acts, bloody initiation rites, and severe punishments that border on torture.

It is now clear that in some instances, the Brothers themselves cultivated some of the myths and even helped to invent tales and half-truths to dissuade prying outsiders from interrupting and disturbing the activities of their moradas.

✛   ✛   ✛

FIGURE 7. *Two maderos against buttress, early morning, summer, 1993.*

I am convinced that many of the Penitente black myths, or legends, about people being nailed to crosses or men being buried up to their neck in sand or cactus whippings were perpetuated by our own Brothers.

The more I study the matter, the more I believe they wanted to purposefully horrify outsiders in order to keep them away. But what happened is that the tactic backfired. The vivid tales drew people to the moradas just like onlookers flock to a car wreck. The element of mystery is always captivating.

AN HERMANO

I do not really like to use the word penance *when speaking of the Brotherhood and our activities at the morada. Every Christian is called to penance. What we do both inside and outside our moradas is something else. We are really sending our little flowers to God—these are our sacrifices.*

We see our faults, but we don't castigate ourselves. Instead, we send our gifts

✛   28

—our flowers, our sacrifices. Our gifts of what some people may call penance are really acts of love.

AN HERMANO

There are several different procedures we do inside our moradas. Some of them I cannot bring up to the public because we believe that whatever we do inside the morada is things we do in remembrance of Christ. Those are done in private.

It is like when a man and a woman get married. The wedding Mass and the party afterward are open and for the public, but you don't go asking the couple about what they did on their wedding night. The bridal suite is private. The same is true with our fraternity.

AN HERMANO

✠   ✠   ✠

Although chapters of the Hermandad flourished throughout the nineteenth century, the Brothers were forced to go underground. This was partly because of the influx of Anglo settlers whose Protestant sensibilities were greatly offended by the lurid tales of self-flagellation and simulated crucifixions.

More problems and threats came for the Brothers in 1851 when Bishop Jean Baptiste Lamy arrived in New Mexico with his fellow French priests. They had little regard for most aspects of the Spanish culture, especially the lay Brotherhood. A cultural clash quickly resulted when Lamy took exception to the beloved santos produced by local craftsmen and had the images removed from churches and chapels.

Lamy, who became archbishop in 1875, truly misunderstood the Hispanic traditions and did everything in his power to manipulate the Hermandad. So did his successor, Archbishop Jean Baptiste Salpointe, another

Frenchman. The result was an authorized set of rules that the Brotherhood continues to use today.

✠   ✠   ✠

We have to admit that Lamy was important to us. If he had not done to us what he did, then maybe we would not have clung to our traditions and beliefs as strongly as we have in order to stay alive. With adversity, you are forced to fight for survival.

AN HERMANO

✠   ✠   ✠

Los Hermanos remained unofficial and out of public view until January 28, 1947, when Archbishop Edwin V. Byrne officially recognized the Hermandad's historic affiliation with the Catholic Church. Byrne gave the Brothers his blessing and commended them for keeping the faith alive for so many years.

In spite of periods when cultural awareness as well as interest and membership in the Brotherhood declined, forcing some chapters to close, the Hermandad has managed to survive. Many Brothers believe their future looks bright. For this to happen, all of the moradas must be preserved and respected.

✠   ✠   ✠

I want people to know that we are not a secret organization. We have always had an open door. We do not hold deep, dark, terrible secrets.

AN HERMANO

The Brotherhood is definitely growing. At one point, it really was going down-hill and becoming stale. Finally, the younger generation snapped to and discovered that our culture was dying. They realized the best way to preserve it was through the morada.

AN HERMANO

History truly does repeat itself. Now we are losing more and more priests here in New Mexico and the church seems to be going through a decline, enduring a real test of its own. There are many problems ahead for the church. It is no coincidence that while that is going on, the Brotherhood is gaining more and more members. I don't find that strange at all. It is very natural.

AN HERMANO

XIII

It was through the law that I have died to the law to live for God. I have been crucified with Christ, and the life I live now is not my own; Christ is living in me. I still live my human life, but it is a life of faith in the Son.

GALATIANS 2:19-20 (NAB)

XIV

Good Friday evening. The door of Morada del Alto is shut to the world outside. All the windows are covered. Worshipers fill the *oratorio,* where the smell of potted lilies, fresh flowers, and burning candles is strong. Flickering shadows play on the walls.

Midnight is coming. The time is at hand for Las Tinieblas, the Darkness. Similar to the Church's Tenebrae service, this is the Brothers' high drama, commemorating the time of darkness that overcame the earth when Christ died on the cross.

At the start of the ceremony, the altar candles are the sole source of light. The candles in the Tenebrae candelabra usually range in number from a dozen to seventeen depending on the particular morada, with the apex candle always standing for Christ. Each morada is autonomous and there are variations in the ceremonies. Brothers at some moradas burn a single white candle representing Christ, and twelve yellow candles symbolizing the disciples. At this morada fourteen candles glow.

Two Hermanos near the altar chant an alabado. At the conclusion of each verse, a candle flame is pinched out. The room becomes darker and darker. As the light slowly leaves, a young girl asks her grandmother why it is growing so dark.

"They are taking away the Light of the World," whispers the old woman. Tears fill her eyes.

One candle after another is snuffed out, signifying how, one by one, the apostles abandoned Jesus. Finally, only the white candle is left. A Brother hides this last candle, and the room is absolutely dark. It means that death has taken Christ.

For an instant, there is utter silence.

Suddenly chaos erupts. From another room comes a thunderous din caused by stamping feet, drums, whirling *matracas,* and the shrill *pito,* or flute. Chains are crashed to the floor, echoes of the cries of souls in purgatory resound. This pandemonium represents the earthquake following Christ's death, when the temple veil was torn and the dead arose.

The morada seems to tremble. It is agony.

Then as suddenly as it began, the cacophony stops. The huddled villagers respond by calling out the names of departed loved ones and reciting *sudarios,* prayers for the dead. The Hermandad is the only Catholic organization that maintains the Jewish tradition of praying for the dead after the service.

At long last, the white candle is returned. It is used to bring the other candles back to life. An alabado is sung.

The villagers take their leave, but the Brothers remain behind. They stay in their morada. They stay to bask in the light, *en divina luz.*

XV

Long after the season of Lent is a memory, La Divina Luz still shimmers. Deep into summer, when the second crop of alfalfa is almost ready to be cut and jars of fresh apricot jam turn up for sale at highway stands, the Divine Light is still there. Those who form the mosaic of the Hermandad know this.

In the Española Valley, past the San Juan Pueblo and just north of Alcalde, a young Brother and his wife walk their land. The ground is littered with history. Thousands of pottery shards and pieces of broken metates, stones used for grinding maize, can be seen everywhere. After a rainstorm, these fragments of long ago erupt from the earth as if to remind those living of the past.

The Brother's small adobe house is atop an ancient dumping ground. A thousand years earlier, this was home for a culture most people have for-

FIGURE 8. *Window and crumbling adobe walls, early afternoon, summer, 1993.*

gotten. But not the Hermano. Since he was a little boy, he has been drawn to this parcel of land. He knows every inch of it and can feel the spirits that dwell in the soil.

Below is the Hacienda de Los Luceros, the remains of the historic San Sebastián Martín Land Grant of 1703. Not far away, the Río Grande runs its course, as does the *acequia madre,* the mother ditch, dug by hand by Native Americans. Water from the acequia quenches the thirsts of fields and orchards from Velarde to San Juan.

The young man realizes that the words of wisdom from one of his older Hermanos are true: water is no good without the earth, and the earth is no good without the water.

⁜   ⁜   ⁜

Both land and water are essential. I wouldn't have this house if it were not for the land and water. This house is made up of both. So is our morada. There is a dependence.

We as Brothers are also dependent. We would not be able to maintain our moradas by ourselves. It takes all the Hermanos and Hermanas. They are my true brothers and sisters. We share our food, our time, and our prayers. We are part of the circle together. We maintain our morada, and at the same time we maintain ourselves.

AN HERMANO

⁜   ⁜   ⁜

The young Brother puts in long hours as a skillful *santero* and bilingual poet. For inspiration, he needs only to look out a window. Before him are the timeless acequia, the Truchas Peaks, and all the heavens.

Twenty-six miles north of Española, on the edge of the ranching community of El Rito, another dedicated *santero* and fellow Hermano also fuels a creative soul by turning to his ancestral land. As a boy, this Brother saw the shapes of animals in the rocks and sticks he discovered in the arroyos and along the banks of the river. He gathered the pieces of wood and stone and brought them home. He carved snakes and birds, but then he saw the faces of saints in the wood. His mother also could see the faces, and she scribbled down a simple verse about her son.

When I go down to the river
To get dry wood for carving
I know God knows
I am working with my heart.

The woman was always pleased that her youngest child possessed a special imagination and talent. She kept it all to herself, and prayed that God would watch over her boy and allow him to see the faces forever.

God heard the woman's prayers. The *santero* Brother still stalks the canyons and forests. He walks among the spirits that dwell in the land, and he gathers wood to use for his bultos. He collects earth and minerals, and he transforms them into natural pigments for coloring his sacred art.

Taught about the bounties of nature by his mother, the *santero* was undergoing initiation into the Hermandad when he was reminded that his own great-uncle was known far and wide as the "Santero de Muerte." He was given this name because of the death figures he carved for several moradas, including the one "on the hill."

When his famous relative's Muerte was damaged in the Morada del Alto fire, the young *santero* made a striking new figure of death to take its place.

He also has reached out to a young nephew. Already an Hermano him-

self, the teenage boy is apprenticed to his uncle—known as the "Santero of El Rito." The tradition stays alive.

✠   ✠   ✠

I knew that God had called upon me to become a santero and to join the Brotherhood. Then to reinforce it, some years ago my car was hit head-on during a snowstorm and my body was thrown through the windshield into a ditch. I lay there covered with snow and wasn't discovered until the next day.

I am sure that I died. I found myself in a tunnel, and it was lit by a heavenly glow. It was a very bright light. And at the end of the tunnel was La Muerte. The Angel of Death was there waiting, but Death did not take me.

God brought me back to give me another chance to do my work—to make saints and to serve my morada.

AN HERMANO

FIGURE 9. *La Muerte, Doña Sebastiana*

✠   ✠   ✠

Every day he draws breath, regardless of the time of year, the Hermano gives thanks to God for allowing him to walk in the divine light.

XVI

Under the brilliant summer sun, the Santa Fe Plaza is filled with saints and archangels. San Miguel, San Rafael, Santa Verónica, San José, San Lorenzo, San Gerónimo, Santa Clara, San Antonio, San Cristóbal, San Pedro, San Francisco de Asís, San Isidro Labrador, Santa Rita, San Gabriel, Santiago,

Santa Bárbara, and a legion of other holy images are assembled in the early morning light. This is God's army, a sacred congregation fashioned from pine, cottonwood root, and aspen. The guardians of soldiers, travelers, orphans, carpenters, animals, crops, families, and many others are all present and ac-counted for.

San Juan Nepomuceno, the patron of silence and secrecy, water, and the Hermandad, as well as a protector against gossip and slander, is on hand. So are Nuestra Señora de Guadalupe and the esteemed Santo Niño de Atocha.

The saints have all come for the Traditional Spanish Market. This annual event has evolved into the oldest and largest showcase for Hispanic artists working in established New Mexican art forms and media. The city's historic plaza is flanked with tables laden with the cherished arts and crafts of hundreds of *santeros, santeras,* tinsmiths, and other artisans.

Brightly painted retablos and bultos, colcha embroidery, weaving, straw appliqué, tinwork, furniture, and pottery are displayed in a silent celebration of this important part of New Mexico's centuries-old living heritage.

Many of the *santeros* and artists gathered on the plaza happen to be Brothers from several moradas. A few of Los Hermanos have received the top awards for their exquisite works.

FIGURE 10. *Santos, left to right: Cristo crucificado (bulto), San Antonio (bulto), Nuestra Señora de Guadalupe (retablo).*

✠ ✠ ✠

We make our santos just like our ancestors did. When we make new santos, we honor God and we honor those who came before us. And when we touch the older statues our ancestors made, then we touch our ancestors.

AN HERMANO

☩   ☩   ☩

One of the Brothers from Morada del Alto sits on a folding chair beneath the portal, or overhanging roof, of the Palace of the Governors on the north side of the plaza. The oldest public building in continuous use in the nation, the adobe fortress, El Palacio Real, has evolved into a tidy museum of history.

Before the *santero* on a table set up below the portal of the Palace of the Governors are some of his prized retablos. He created them in the crowded workshop at his Santa Fe home during the long months of winter and spring.

On most days, the Native Americans from the distant Río Grande pueblos line this shaded sidewalk and sell their pottery and handcrafted turquoise and silver jewelry. But on this summer weekend, the native people quietly relinquish their place on the plaza to their Hispanic brothers and sisters.

Earlier in the summer, a teenager speeding through the plaza lost control of his vehicle. The automobile careened into the portal's thick support timbers, knocking down a long section of the roof. When the repair crews began their work, they discovered that dry rot had spread throughout the portal.

The Hermano and his wife cannot help but smile when they glance up at the workmen's scaffolding still in place, and at the portions of the roof being repaired, draped in sheets of plastic.

⊹　⊹　⊹

We always try to remember that good can come from bad. If it wasn't for that teenage kid out on a joyride who knocked down the portal, then they would not have discovered the rot and all the problems beneath. The wood looked so strong, but it wasn't strong at all. If that accident wouldn't have happened, then perhaps a flock of tourists might have been there looking at jewelry on the sidewalk and the entire roof could have fallen down on them and killed or injured everyone.

That is why the wrecking of the portal is just like what happened at our morada. When that evil came along and burned down our morada, everyone—the whole community and all of the Hermanos and the people of northern New Mexico—pulled together and united as one. As we always say, things happen for a reason.

WIFE OF AN HERMANO

⊹　⊹　⊹

Across the plaza from the Palace of the Governors sits the Woolworth's department store, an unassuming edifice completely surrounded by stylish boutiques and exclusive galleries.

Some of the old-time Santa Feans believe that the Woolworth's, smelling of popcorn and soda-fountain treats and loaded with inexpensive wares, just might be the last authentic business remaining in the entire downtown historic district. A few of the Brothers who have come to Santa Fe from their outland homes are in agreement.

They also hold that there is yet another significant purpose for the Woolworth's besides accommodating the shopping public, as it has since 1925. They point out that in the creation of many rugs and blankets, traditional designs emerge from the weaver's memory—always with a break or an intentional flaw in the pattern so the maker's spirit can go free. The Brothers contend that the Woolworth's serves as Santa Fe's escape hatch, allowing some of the residue, or social pollution, caused by trendy commercialism to drift out of Santa Fe and fade far away in the clear summer skies.

Close by the venerable Woolworth's, the Hermano known for creating death angels from wood watches the crowd of inquisitive *turistas* and the parade of local citizens shuffling past his array of bultos. The passers-by seem especially drawn to the large Muerte that the Brother has carved from cottonwood. This figure has human hair, and its eyes are made of mica. The Muerte holds a pine bow, and a crown of tin sits on its skull.

A few yards from the Muerte, at another table, is the older Brother who carves tool handles, rings, and neckerchief slides from the bones of sheep and deer. He is accompanied by members of his family, and they have laid out some of his best shepherd's ivory for all to see.

Nearby sits another Hermano's wife behind a display of clay pots flecked with mica and hand-polished to a luster. This pottery is made in the traditional method, with clay dug from ancient pits. The woman was taught to make the pottery by an Hermano who is equally proud of his Hispanic and Jicarilla Apache ancestry.

Later in the summer, a woman marking her birthday will be presented with one of the Brother's pottery seed jars, formed from the earth that makes adobes for homes, churches, and moradas. The gift of the earthen vessel will remind her that when one sows seeds in life on behalf of others, it is important to reserve a few seeds to plant in one's own behalf.

✠   ✠   ✠

To be true Hermanos means we have to learn how to give to others and to ourselves. We need to be able to make sacrifices. We should be willing to give of our time, talent, and treasure.

AN HERMANO

⊹   ⊹   ⊹

FIGURE 11. *Jicarilla seed jar*

Beneath the shade trees in the heart of the plaza park are the young exhibitors of the Spanish Market. They represent the next generation—youngsters who are interested in preserving traditional Hispanic arts and crafts as well as the culture of their ancestors. They are the children and grandchildren of respected elder *santeros.* Some of them come from families which have always maintained an association with the Hermandad. At least one of these young people is a Brother.

The teenage nephew of the *santero* who carries on the tradition of carving death angels sits in the middle of the plaza. The young man's round face is framed in the sun's glow by his retablos and bultos. In the midst of his santos stands a solitary figure of death about a foot tall. She is covered with black cloth and a veil, and her striking eyes were taken from a strand of costume-jewelry pearls. In her smiling mouth is a single tooth. The youngster grins when he admits the tooth is his own. A man who realizes the young *santero's* dark angel is special gently lifts the Muerte from the table. She has found a home. That afternoon, the shrouded figure will go to live in a place of prominence in a small house in the Barrio de Analco,

41 ⊹

the oldest neighborhood in the city south of the Santa Fe River. The young Hermano is pleased. He understands that when he is an old man, after a lifetime of carving saints and other images from cottonwood, the Muerte with pearl eyes and his own baby tooth in her gaping mouth will still be smiling.

✝ ✝ ✝

I care about tradition. I do what I can to keep our traditions alive. I want to encourage other kids to try doing this work, and also to become involved with the Brotherhood and the moradas so that our traditions won't go away.

 We need to not only preserve our arts, but our religion. That is why our moradas are so important.

AN HERMANO

✝ ✝ ✝

Early on the Sabbath of the Spanish Market, a mariachi Mass is conducted. The service is held just a block east of the plaza at the Saint Francis Cathedral, built by Archbishop Lamy in a Romanesque style to remind him of his native France. Lamy's old bones are in a crypt under the altar. In front of the cathedral, in the shadows of the twin flat-topped towers, stands the archbishop's bronze statue, peering down San Francisco Street like a mute sentinel.

 Stained-glass windows made by French artisans line the nave of this cathedral. It was built not of adobe but of golden brown New Mexican sandstone that stonemasons from Italy quarried at Arroyo Sais, Lamy Junction, and La Bajada Mesa. Chimes sound. White candles glow, and sunshine seeps through the high windows. Worshipers fill all the smooth wooden pews. Many of the women, their heads covered in lace mantillas, clutch rosaries. Old gentlemen kneel and pray. A priest in white vestments marches down the long aisle, bearing a cross adorned with eagle feathers.

Behind him are two Hermanos. One is the *santero* from El Rito who likes to create Muertes. He is carrying one of his carvings. It is the crucified Christ. The other Hermano is the man's young nephew, with one of his own retablos cradled in his arms.

The worshipers rise in silence. By the time the procession reaches the altar, a sweet mariachi serenade of guitar and violin echoes throughout the cathedral and spills outside. Not a single word of French is uttered, and only a little English. Almost the entire mass—the prayers, the hymns, the Holy Communion—is said in Spanish.

✠   ✠   ✠

This is not Archbishop Lamy's church. It really never was his church. It is a cathedral for all the people. Lamy is dead and gone. We remain. The Hermandad is alive.

AN HERMANO

✠   ✠   ✠

As soon as the mass has concluded, the procession leaves the cathedral. This time, it is joined by the mariachis, with red sashes tied around their waists. The long line of clerics, musicians, and Brothers exits through the large cathedral doors. Without noticing it, they walk past the statue of Lamy to the plaza for the blessing of the Spanish Market. They march past La Fonda, the hotel at the end of the Santa Fe Trail. When they enter the crowded plaza, the songs of the cathedral bells are heard.

The two Hermanos, still holding their sacred art, stand proudly as the blessing is delivered. The mariachis resume their music. A shower of sunlight pours through the trees and engulfs the plaza. The light covers wooden saints and archangels lining the streets.

Soft smiles bud on the mouths of the Hermanos. It is the most fitting benediction.

XVII

Throughout northern New Mexico lofty cottonwoods flourish. These are trees that give shade, feed fires, and sometimes become santos. Familiar sights along roads and acequias, cottonwoods grow near marshy places called ciénegas, and they form bosques, the groves fringing rivers and mountain streams.

FIGURE 12. *Cottonwood trees, late autumn, near La Cienega, 1988.*

In summer, female trees yield snowstorms of cotton, and the foliage creates a liquid whisper in the wind. When autumn visits the land and clusters of fall-blooming chamiso flowers go bright yellow and lemon gold, the heart-shaped cottonwood leaves follow suit.

Days grow shorter as winter comes around. The leaves turn loose and fall to become one with the earth.

Long after the last chile crop has been harvested and hung up to dry and the cut piñon wood has been stacked outside many mountain homes, the naked limbs and furrowed trunks of the great silvery white cottonwood specters stand out in stark contrast against the cold blue sky.

While the earth slumbers through frigid days and nights, the enduring sunlight keeps hope alive for the Brothers in the cities and villages.

✠　✠　✠

The night is far spent; the day draws near. Let us cast off deeds of darkness and put on the armor of light.

ROMANS 13:12 (NAB)

✠　✠　✠

Throughout the long months of winter, the Brothers continue their work. Their vigil never ceases; the reenactment of the mysteries of salvation does not end. They pray for the sick, help bury the dead, and care for widows and orphans. They wage battle against despair.

They know that when the sap rises, the snowbanks will melt into the rivers, and once again alfalfa seeds will sprout in the adobe soil. They are confident that the divine light will remain steadfast and will give them victory over the darkness. It is simply a matter of faith.

✠　✠　✠

We are brokers of knowledge among our own people. We are the keepers of the flame. Many devices are used to ensure that our Hispanic traditions remain alive—song, dance, language, and arts. But our moradas are the most important bastions for preserving our way of life. Inside the morada, all of us will continue. The moradas are our salvation and our hope.

AN HERMANO

✠　✠　✠

The Photographs

3.

2. Finished stone morada with round-ended apse, late afternoon light, early summer, 1993.
Light sequence, plates 2 – 5.

Por ser mi divina luz
ay, Jesús del alma mía
llevando en mi compañía
a nuestro Padre Jesús.

Los que creyen en la iglesia
y en esta divina luz
serán de los verdaderos
de nuestro Padre Jesús.

1. Door detail with light from setting sun,
afternoon, late winter, 1990.

For you are my divine light
O Jesus of my soul
carrying in my company
our Father Jesus.

Those who believe in the church
and in this divine light
will be among the true ones
of our Father Jesus.

FROM THE ALABADO
Por Ser Mi Divina Luz
(For You Are My Divine Light)

6. Cross on tree outside door of vandalized morada, late afternoon, spring, 1990.

7. Cross and clearing storm over mountains, dawn, early winter, 1990.

8. Shutter and adobe detail on morada, afternoon, early spring, 1990.

9. Morada and low-lying clouds, late afternoon light, summer, 1993.

10. Approaching thunderstorm and abandoned morada, afternoon light, autumn, 1992.

11. The Blessed Virgin Mary on interior wall of abandoned morada, 1992.

12. Camposanto and fallen tree limbs behind morada, early afternoon, summer, 1993.

13. Morada and three pine trees, early afternoon, summer, 1993.

14. Maderos in afternoon light, late autumn, 1993.

15. Paneled door of kitchen outbuilding, morning, summer, 1993.

16. Cross made of palm frond on shutter of kitchen outbuilding, morning, summer, 1993.

17. Calvario in snow, morning, winter, 1992.

Más hermosa que la luna,
más linda que el sol eres;
desde el principio del mundo,
Señora, bendita tú eres.

Lovelier than the moon are you
and more beautiful than the sun;
from the beginning of the world,
Lady, you are blest.

FROM THE ALABADO
"Dios te salve, Bella Aurora"
(Hail [God Save You] Beautiful Dawn)

18. Moonrise over morada, dusk, late autumn, 1991.

19. Door of old plastered adobe morada, afternoon, early spring, 1990.

20. Morada after the fire with devil's pentagram (taken the day after), afternoon, autumn, 1992.

21. Morada, tennis courts, and approaching storm, early afternoon, summer, 1993.

22. Morada doors and bench, mid-afternoon, summer, 1993.

23. Approaching thunderstorm over morada and camposanto, mid-afternoon, summer, 1993.

24. Abandoned morada and approaching storm, late afternoon, summer, 1993.

25. Maderos, dawn, summer, 1990.

26. Chiseled cross and letter A detail on side of finished stone morada, afternoon, autumn, 1993.

27. Morada after early winter storm, dawn, 1992.

28. Morada, mesa, and grasses, first morning light, autumn, 1993.

Sus murallas primorosas
admiran con su riqueza,
y con hermosura pasman
y hechizan con su belleza.

Heaven's precious walls,
astonish by their opulence,
by their beauty they astound,
and they bewitch by their loveliness.

FROM THE ALABADO
"Mira Mira Pecador"
(Look, Look, Sinner)

29. Finished stone Penitente chapel with inset plaques and cross, late afternoon light, late autumn, 1993.

30. Cristo and cross, morning, winter, 1992.

31. Two white crosses and shutter, afternoon, autumn, 1992.

32. Morada below rock face and approaching rainstorm, mid-morning, autumn, 1993.

33. Calvario against mountains, evening light, summer, 1992.

34. Morada overlooking church, late afternoon, summer, 1991.

35. Clearing storm clouds, morada, camposanto, and calvario, late afternoon, 1990.

¡Cielo y tierra, aplaudid,
alabando a nuestro Dios!
¡Santos, ángeles, rendidos
a nuestro Dios y Señor!

Heaven and earth, clap
in praise of our God!
Saints and angels, give yourselves
to our God and Lord!

FROM THE ALABADO
"Amoroso Nos Convida"
(Lovingly He Invites Us)

36. Morada with separate Penitente chapel (left) and meeting house, afternoon, summer, 1993.

37. Standing maderos and gravestone, vandalized morada, late afternoon, spring, 1990.

38. Vandalized morada, late afternoon, spring, 1990.

39. Crosses of Calvary, the llano, and distant thunderclouds, afternoon, summer, 1993.

40. Morada overlooking valley, last light, summer, 1993.

41. White cross and door, morada, morning, late winter, 1990.

42. Morada and cross, first morning light, summer, 1993.

43. Cross with stapled palm-frond cross on door of kitchen outbuilding, morning, summer, 1993.

44. Tenth Station of the Cross, late afternoon, early winter, 1993.

El sol ya se ha oscurecido
la tierra se ve temblando.
El velo se va rasgando
y las piedras hacen ruido.
El mundo está conmovido
cuando muere el Salvador.

The sun has darkened
and the earth is quaking.
The veil [of the temple] is tearing
the rocks even make noise.
The whole world is moved to pity
when the Savior dies.

CORO

Por tu pasión Jesús Mío,
Abrázame en vuestro Amor.

CHORUS

By your passion my Jesus
Embrace me in your love.

FROM THE ALABADO
"La Pasión"
(The Passion)

45. Morada after summer rainstorm, morning, 1992.

46. Camposanto overlooking morada, dawn, early autumn, 1993.

47. Morada and white hills, morning, autumn, 1993.

48. Window blackened by fire and fallen shutter (taken the day after), afternoon, autumn, 1992.

49. Linear morada, early afternoon, summer, 1992.

50. Approaching storm over Via Crucis (Way of the Cross), late afternoon, spring, 1994.

51. Stone morada with belfry, early afternoon, spring, 1994.

52. Four crosses on end of vigas and door detail, afternoon, autumn, 1993.

53. Morada with calvario on hillside, and afternoon stormclouds, early autumn, 1993.

54. Approaching thunderstorm over cruciform morada, afternoon, autumn, 1990.

55. White cross and morada, morning, late winter, 1990.

56. Morada and last light of day, early autumn, 1992.

57. Morada after snowstorm, dusk, winter, 1990.

Despues de esta despedida
con sus discípulos fue
desde la ciudad al huerto
donde ha orado otra vez.

After this farewell
He left with His disciples
from the city to the garden
where He had prayed before.

FROM THE ALABADO
Con Mansedumbre y Ternura
(With Mild Tenderness)

58. Kneeling Cristo, mid-afternoon, summer, 1991.

59. Morada with bell tower, late afternoon, early winter, 1990.

60. Crosses over door depicting the Fourteen Stations of the Cross, morning, spring, 1990.

61. Vandalized morada, maderos, and a Station of the Cross, late afternoon, spring, 1993.

62. Morada and stormclouds, mid-afternoon, summer, 1993.

63. Door with cross detail, morning, summer, 1993.

64. Rebuilt morada and maderos, dawn, summer, 1993.

65. Camposanto in cottonwood grove near morada, evening light, summer, 1993.

66. Morada, Cristo, and camposanto, evening light, late autumn, 1992.

Nunca es noche, siempre es día
en esa hermosa ciudad,
porque la luz que le alumbra
es de Dios su claridad.

It is never night, always day
in that beautiful city,
for the light that illuminates it
is the splendor of God.

67. Cruciform morada and family chapel on hill, late afternoon, autumn, 1990.

Afterword

The ancient tradition of singing to welcome the dawn, the first light of day, is still very much a part of the Lenten rituals practiced by my Penitente Brothers. Across the forested mountains, cottonwood-lined rivers, dry arroyo canyons and piñon-studded hills of this land of my ancestors, we greet the new day for all it has to offer, singing

Bendito sea	*Blessed be*
la luz del día,	*the light of the day*
bendito sea	*blessed be He*
quien nos la envía.	*that sends it to us.*

This book, *En Divina Luz,* challenges you, the viewer, to see the Penitente Brotherhood and our sacred buildings with your heart and to listen with your eyes. The humble buildings that my people call moradas are shown here with a dignity and in a light never before presented. The text, with its emphasis on my people, reaffirms the spirit that envelops the moradas and the ritual cycle created within and outside their timeless walls.

For the past twenty years I have watched many of the old moradas fall into disrepair. The condition of many reflects the economic and social conditions of the Hispanic villages where they are found. The people who once devotedly cared for these sacred structures have moved away, grown old, or passed on. Still, we try to keep our moradas alive and in good repair.

My soul wept the morning of September 17, 1992, as I gazed at the burned-out remains of the morada of which I have been a member for the past fifteen Lenten seasons. Our beloved two-hundred-year-old structure was vandalized and burned. The morada's historic contents, including our beloved santos, centuries-old manuscripts, and other religious paraphernalia, were destroyed or damaged. As I knelt in the smoldering ashes, I asked God to forgive the perpetrators and then vowed to rebuild the morada. The thought that my two children would never be blessed with the experience of praying in the morada of their Penitente ancestors, of never lifting their eyes to the santos on the altar or chanting the centuries-old alabados, terrified me. In the worst winter in the past thirty years, we rebuilt our morada. It was dedicated on Viernes de Dolores (Friday of Sorrows), the feast of our patron saint, Nuestra Señora de Dolores (Our Lady of Sorrows), one week before Easter Sunday 1993.

My irrevocable petition to the Crucified Christ is that this morada will never again have to be rebuilt anew, that it will be maintained and loved until the time comes when it will be reclaimed by Mother Earth. The spirit of the morada is alive once again. The destruction was by the hand of man. In recent years several moradas have been destroyed by uncaring individuals. Other moradas have slowly melted back into the earth from where they often came. This book reminds us of the life cycles of these sacred buildings.

When I tell the history of my people, I often speak of moradas as being full of memory, the memory of the Passion and death of Jesus Christ, of all the Hermanos Penitentes who came before, of the countless flickering candles that have lit darkened interiors, of prayers on beaded rosaries, of sad alabados, of tears, and of bent knees resting on sacred ground. A glimpse of these memories can be found in this book. It is my prayer that this presentation in pictures and words, like the dawn of new light, will bring a better understanding of my people, the Hispanic Penitente Brotherhood of New Mexico, and that it will teach respect for our moradas, thereby ensuring their preservation.

HERMANO CHARLES M. CARRILLO
Hermano de la Morada de Nuestra Señora de Dolores del Alto
January 1994

Author's Note

Since my early twenties, I have carried on a passionate love affair with New Mexico. That is why no matter how far I stray I always return. Each year close to Easter I come back in remembrance of the rites of Los Hermanos that I was first fortunate to witness quietly during Lenten seasons long past.

I realize I will never be free of the powerful spell of observing a scheme of life geared to celebrating with humble passion the religious as well as the agricultural year. I have been allowed to participate in history. For that experience I am forever grateful.

When I was a struggling young writer a quarter of a century ago, New Mexico gifted me with extraordinary mentors and nurtured my creative soul until by right of experience I could claim the craft of writing as my own.

It is my hope that my words contained in this book, combined with the voices of the Brothers themselves and the exquisite images created by Craig Varjabedian, will serve as a lasting tribute to the Hermandad and their moradas.

MICHAEL WALLIS
Santa Fe, New Mexico
November 1993

Photographer's Note

"He was not the light, only a witness to speak for the light."
JOHN 1:8 (JB)

My earliest encounter with a morada was a profound experience. It happened late one afternoon on an early winter day. I remember driving into a small village north of Santa Fe as if directed by an unknown hand. The road wound up and around a cluster of homes and brought me to the top of a hill overlooking the village and its fields. There I found a structure with a powerful presence.

The light that day was simply spectacular. Swirling clouds covered the sky and for a moment obscured the low, setting sun. For a minute or two it began to snow, and I still can remember the sensation of sharp frozen crystals of ice stinging my face. As the sun emerged from below the clouds, the light illuminated the snow shower so that it looked like millions of tiny shooting stars falling to earth. The clouds continued to swirl in the sky and obscured the sun once more. It became very quiet and still.

I was carried from this unfolding moment into a meditative state where quiet emotions seemed to take over all perceptions and to make them appear otherworldly. Spellbound, I watched the moon rise over this powerful structure on the hill and above the valley around. Time seemed frozen as light danced across distant mountain peaks and dark clouds loomed overhead. The moon continued on its path across the heavens, the glow from its mantle seen briefly through the few pockets of clear sky. I became a witness to a landscape that appeared to be illuminated by a light emanating from inside this morada rather than from the setting sun. This light gave warmth despite the dropping temperature and determined gusts of wind. When the snow began to fall again, I knew that an important gift had been given to me.

It was ice crystals being carried on the wind and striking my face once again that brought me back to the present. Wanting to capture the essence of this fleeting moment, I tried to set up my camera, but the sun had already retreated over the distant hillside. Reflecting on the experience while driving home, I found myself left with questions. If it was my destiny to receive such gifts while making photographs, I concluded it would be through the lens of my camera that an answer might reveal itself. So began a photographic journey across New Mexico to follow the light.

A grant from the Samuel H. Kress Foundation in 1990 provided me support to photograph for approximately one year. Later I received two generous grants from the National Endowment for the Arts which together with support from other sources allowed me to continue exploring with my camera these humble structures built as bridges between the everyday and the transcendent. It is an involvement that has spanned several years, covered many miles, and resulted in a lot of photographs.

My own desire to make these pictures was not to expose any of the private devotions that take place inside the morada. Instead, I wanted to create images that engaged my own feelings and emotions regarding these simple buildings where through the light, the Creator makes His presence known. While making pictures at other moradas, I witnessed the light again and again, and sometimes it illuminated subtleties that might have been missed because rational thinking considered them unimportant. The light was becoming my teacher. It could reveal the quintessential moment to release the shutter on my camera, to open a door if you will, which would allow forms riding on waves of light to pass freely and manifest themselves on film. Also, it taught me how to explore within my own process the powerful emotions about my own relationship with the Divine which seemed to surface in the presence of these sacred buildings. Intuitively, I came to understand through making these photographs that while I could never *be* the light, I could, as a photographer, be a witness to speak *for* the light. My photographs are presented along with Michael Wallis' words as statements to that end.

As you experience these images you may note that none of the titles contains information with which to locate any of the moradas. If it is indeed true that being a Penitente Brother is a private commitment made to honor and walk with the Creator, then too, I believe the locations of their walks must remain private as well.

Each morada represents the human soul's longing for a direct experience with the Divine. While many moradas were built by Hermanos years ago as places of worship and brotherhood, they are testimony to us all that Spirit, in whatever form we believe it to take, can still be found today. These sacred buildings are reminders, too, that in the remote mountain villages of northern New Mexico and southern Colorado, groups of men and their families continue to live lives bathed in the light of the Divine.

CRAIG VARJABEDIAN
Santa Fe, New Mexico
January 1994

Selected Bibliography

The Penitente Brotherhood, Moradas, and Alabados

Ahlborn, Richard E. *Penitente Moradas of Abiquiú.* Washington, D.C.: Smithsonian, 1968, 1986.

Aranda, Charles. *The Penitente Papers.* Albuquerque: Charles Aranda, 1974.

Briggs, Charles L. *Competence in Performance: The Creativity of Tradition in Mexicano Verbal Art.* Philadelphia: University of Pennsylvania Press, 1988.

Bunting, Bainbridge, Thomas R. Lyons, and Margil Lyons. "Penitente Brotherhood Moradas and their Architecture." In *Hispanic Arts and Ethnohistory in the Southwest,* edited by Marta Weigle, pp. 30-79. Albuquerque: University of New Mexico Press, 1983.

Chavez, Fray Angélico. *My Penitente Land.* Albuquerque: University of New Mexico Press, 1974. Reprinted, Santa Fe: Museum of New Mexico Press, 1993.

Córdova, Lorenzo de. *Echoes of the Flute.* Notes by Marta Weigle. Santa Fe: Ancient City Press, 1972.

Kernberger, Karl and Craig Varjabedian. *En Divina Luz,* "Colores!" No. 207. 28 minutes. KNME-TV5, Albuquerque, New Mexico, 1990. Videocassette of television program.

Lyons, Thomas, and Marta Weigle. "Brothers and Neighbors." In *Celebration,* edited by Victor Turner, pp. 231-51. Washington, D.C.: Smithsonian, 1982.

Mills, George, and Richard Grove. *Lucifer and the Crucifer.* Colorado Springs: Taylor Museum, 1966.

Music of New Mexico: Hispanic Traditions. Produced by Howard Bass. Compact disc SF 40409. Smithsonian Folkways, 1992.

Rael, Juan B. *The New Mexican* Alabado. Stanford: Stanford University Press, 1951. Reprinted, New York: AMS Press, 1967.

Robb, John Donald. *Hispanic Folk Music of New Mexico and the Southwest.* Norman: University of Oklahoma Press, 1980.

Steele, Thomas J., S.J., and Rowena A. Rivera. *Penitente Self-Government: Brotherhoods and Councils, 1797-1947.* Santa Fe: Ancient City Press, 1985.

Tate, Bill. *Penitentes of the Sangre de Cristos.* Las Truchas, New Mexico: Tate Gallery, 1966.

Weigle, Marta. *Brothers of Light, Brothers of Blood: The Penitentes of the Southwest.* Albuquerque: University of New Mexico Press, 1976. Reprinted, Santa Fe: Ancient City Press, 1989.

———. *Penitente Bibliography.* Albuquerque: University of New Mexico Press, 1976.

Woodward, Dorothy. *The Penitentes of New Mexico.* Ph.D. Dissertation, Yale University, 1935. Reprinted, New York: Arno Press, 1974.

New Mexico

Brown, Lorin W., with Charles L. Briggs and Marta Weigle. *Hispano Folklife of New Mexico: The Lorin W. Brown Federal Writers' Project Manuscripts.* Albuquerque: University of New Mexico Press, 1978.

Coles, Robert, and Alex Harris. *The Old Ones of New Mexico.* Albuquerque: University of New Mexico Press, 1973.

Crawford, Stanley. Mayordomo: *Chronicle of an Acequia in Northern New Mexico.* Albuquerque: University of New Mexico Press, 1988.

deBuys, William, and Alex Harris. *River of Traps: A Village Life.* Albuquerque: University of New Mexico Press, 1990.

Warren, Nancy Hunter. *Villages of Hispanic New Mexico.* Santa Fe: School of American Research Press, 1987.

Weber, David J. *The Spanish Frontier in North America.* New Haven and London: Yale University Press, 1992.

Weigle, Marta, ed. *Hispanic Arts and Ethnohistory in the Southwest.* Albuquerque: University of New Mexico Press, 1983.

——— and Peter White. *The Lore of New Mexico.* Albuquerque: University of New Mexico Press, 1988.

Religious Art

Awalt, Barbe, and Paul Rhetts. *Charlie Carrillo: Tradition and Soul.* Albuquerque: LPD Enterprises, 1994.

Boyd, E. *Popular Arts of Spanish New Mexico.* Santa Fe: Museum of New Mexico Press, 1974.

Espinosa, José E. *Saints in the Valley.* Albuquerque: University of New Mexico Press, 1960.

Frank, Larry. *New Kingdom of the Saints: Religious Art of New Mexico 1780-1907.* Santa Fe: Red Crane Books, 1992.

Shalkop, Robert L. *Wooden Saints: The Santos of New Mexico.* Colorado Springs: Taylor Museum and Colorado Springs Fine Arts Center, 1967.

Steele, Thomas J., S.J. Santos *and Saints: The Religious Folk Art of Hispanic New Mexico.* Albuquerque: Calvin Horn, 1974. Reprinted, Santa Fe: Ancient City Press, 1994.

Wroth, William. *Images of Penance, Images of Mercy: Southwestern* Santos *in the Late Nineteenth Century.* Norman: University of Oklahoma Press, 1991.

Acknowledgments

One of the greatest satisfactions in looking back on a journey of many miles is remembering with gratitude the people who helped make the journey a little easier.

Our sincere gratitude and thanks to: Los Hermanos Penitentes, especially Hermanos Charles Carrillo, Floyd Trujillo, and Felipe Ortega for their ever-present, ever-patient counsel, and Hermanos Florencio Gonzales, Nicholas Herrera, Dexter Trujillo, Jacob Trujillo, Jimmy Trujillo, Leopoldo Martinez, and Jake Serna—your kindness, generosity, perceptive minds, and humble faith have served as examples of all that people might become and all that people should strive to be; Debbie B. Carrillo and Virginia S. Trujillo for opinions on the Brotherhood from the woman's point of view.

Kathryn Varjabedian and Suzanne Fitzgerald Wallis for love, patience, and encouragement; Cindy Lane for assistance in making the book and exhibition prints and for being a terrific friend; Thomas J. Steele, S.J., for sensitive advice, assistance, friendship, and fine scholarship; the late Thomas R. Lyons, the pioneer researcher of the Penitente Brotherhood and their moradas and especially his wife Margil for access to unpublished material and patient help when it was most needed; Clark Kimball for seeing the possibilities of combining the abilities of the photographer and author; Michael Carlisle for assistance and support; Kellen Kee McIntyre for organizing and curating the traveling exhibition of the photographs titled "En Divina Luz."

The Santa Fe Council for the Arts and the Western States Arts Federation, for fiscal sponsorship of the Morada Photographic Survey; the Samuel H. Kress Foundation, the Peter and Madeleine Martin Foundation for the Creative Arts, the Marshall L. and Perrine D. McCune Charitable Foundation, the National Endowment for the Arts, the New Mexico Arts Division, the New Mexico Endowment for the Humanities, and several anonymous supporters for providing generous financial assistance; Conservation Resources International, Inc. and William K. Hollinger, Jr. for the contribution of superior archival materials; KNME-TV5, the public television affiliate in Albuquerque and Karl Kernberger and Dale Kruczic for making "En Divina Luz" a part of the award-winning television program *Colores!;* James Moore, John Grassham and the staff at the Albuquerque Museum who contributed to the exhibition; the University of New Mexico Press for making this the finest book possible; Paul Caponigro for proving through photography that rare moments of harmony with the spirit continue to be possible.

Rudolf Arnheim; Adrián Bustamante; Estrellita de Atocha Nichole Carrillo; Roán Miguel Carrillo; Ron Chavez; Emily Dahlgren and Stephen Figliozzi; Phil Davis; the Reverend Nancy Deever; Dixie Haas Dooley; Douglas George; Victor Grant; Beth Hadas; the Reverend Kathleen Jiménez; Tina Kachele; Governor Bruce King; Enrique Lamadrid; Katrina Lasko; John Lucas; Martín Martínez; Hazel Rowena Mills; Therese Mulligan; the late Beaumont Newhall; Craig Newbill; Charles Strong and Mag Diamond; the late Belen Trujillo; Debbie Trujillo; Virgil Trujillo; Hazel Varjabedian; Marta Weigle; Lydia Wyckoff; and Richard Zakia.

Mil gracias a todos

CRAIG VARJABEDIAN

MICHAEL WALLIS